J-P
WAS

Feb01

Santella, Andrew
George Washington

George Washington

by Andrew Santella

Compass Point Early Biographies

Content Adviser: Professor Sherry L. Field,
Department of Social Science Education, College of Education,
The University of Georgia

Reading Adviser: Dr. Linda D. Labbo,
Department of Reading Education, College of Education,
The University of Georgia

 COMPASS POINT BOOKS

Minneapolis, Minnesota

Compass Point Books
3722 West 50th Street, #115
Minneapolis, MN 55410

Visit Compass Point Books on the Internet at *www.compasspointbooks.com* or e-mail your
request to *custserv@compasspointbooks.com*

Photographs ©:
David Bartruff /FPG International, cover; FPG International, cover; Archive Photos, 4; American Stock /Archive Photos, 7;
Archive Photos, 8 top; FPG International, 8 bottom; North Wind Picture Archives, 9; Archive Photos, 10, 11; North Wind
Picture Archives, 13, 14; FPG International, 15; North Wind Picture Archives, 16, 17; Archive Photos, 18, 19;
FPG International, 20; North Wind Picture Archives, 21 top; Archive Photos, 21 bottom; North Wind Picture Archives,
22, 23; Archive Photos, 24; North Wind Picture Archives/Nancy Carter, 25; North Wind Archive Pictures, 26.

Editors: E. Russell Primm and Emily J. Dolbear
Photo Researcher: Svetlana Zhurkina
Photo Selector: Dawn Friedman
Design: Bradfordesign, Inc.

Library of Congress Cataloging-in-Publication Data

Santella, Andrew.
    George Washington / by Andrew Santella.
        p. cm.—(Compass Point early biographies)
    Includes bibliographical references and index.
    Summary: A brief biography of Virginia farm boy who grew up to lead the American army in the
Revolutionary War and become the first president of the United States.
    ISBN 0-7565-0014-1
        1. Washington, George, 1732–1799—Juvenile literature. 2. Presidents—United States—
Biography—Juvenile literature. [1. Washington, George, 1732–1799. 2. Presidents.] I. Title. II. Series.
    E312.66 .S284 2000
    973.4'1'092—dc21   00-008638

Table of Contents

Son of a Farmer

George Washington was born on February 22, 1732, in Virginia. He was the oldest son of a rich farmer named Augustine Washington and his second wife, Mary Ball. George was part of a large family. He had two sisters and three brothers. He also had two older half-brothers.

◄ In a popular but untrue story, young George cannot lie to his father about chopping down a cherry tree.

Young George

George started school when he was seven.
In school, he did well in arithmetic. But his
handwriting needed work. He had to practice
copying a book over and over to improve
his writing.

When George was eleven, his father died.
George's half-brother, Lawrence, helped to
raise George. They lived in a house on the
Potomac River. The house was called Mount
Vernon. Lawrence had been in the British
Navy. George loved hearing his brother's
stories about life at sea. George thought he
might like to be a sailor.

Learning to Be a Surveyor

At the same time, George was learning about being a surveyor. A **surveyor** uses math to measure the size and shape of a piece of land. Because many **settlers** were moving west to find new land, people needed surveyors. When George was just sixteen, he took a trip to the wild country in Virginia with some surveyors. In his diary, he wrote that he slept under a thin blanket full of bedbugs. When he was seventeen, George became a surveyor in Virginia.

George working as a surveyor

Two years later, Lawrence became ill and died. It was up to George to run Mount Vernon. He also joined Virginia's army.

◄ George at age eighteen

As a young soldier ►

The French and Indian War

In 1754, the French and British fought a war in America. This was called the French and Indian War. Washington was soon leading the British troops.

In one battle, his coat was shot through with bullet holes but he was not hurt. The war ended in 1763, and the British won.

George Washington's attack on the French

George Washington was now a well-known and respected army officer.

Life with Martha

In the meantime, George Washington met Martha Custis. They were married on January 6, 1759. George lived with Martha in Mount Vernon. George began improving the house and land. He added to the house and built a **mill**. He also bought more land and planted wheat and corn.

George and Martha's home was called Mount Vernon.

◀ George's wedding to Martha Custis

Serving the People

In 1759, Washington was elected to the House of Burgesses—the government for the **colony** of Virginia. By this time, Britain and the American colonies were having problems. Many Americans believed that Britain was treating the colonies badly.

By 1774, the colonies decided to meet in Philadelphia, Pennsylvania, to discuss these problems. George Washington attended the meeting, called the First Continental Congress. The Congress protested to the British, but the problems remained.

The First Continental Congress met at Carpenter's Hall in Philadelphia.

In 1775, war broke out between Britain and the colonies. The first battles were fought at Lexington and Concord in Massachusetts.

Becoming a Leader

That summer, George Washington returned to Philadelphia for the Second Continental Congress. This time, he wore his blue army uniform. By then, the Congress was looking for a leader to head their army. Colonel George

George Washington taking command of the army

Washington was the natural choice. He was made a general and leader of the entire army.

Leading the army meant fighting against the British, of course. But it also meant persuading the colonies to work together.

14

George goes into battle on horseback. ➤

The Revolutionary War

The Revolutionary War lasted eight years. For much of that time, General George Washington's army lacked food, clothing, and guns. During the winter of 1777–1778, the troops suffered through bitter cold. Many soldiers didn't even have shoes. But George Washington never gave up. He **drilled** his troops. He asked the Congress for better pay

In this famous painting, General Washington crosses the Delaware River in winter.

and supplies for his men. Somehow, he was able to hold the army together.

Year after year, George Washington struggled against the British army. He won enough battles to wear down the British.

The British in defeat

Finally, in 1781, his army, with the help of the French, defeated the British. That battle took place at Yorktown in Virginia. The colonies had finally won independence. Now they were the new United States.

After the War

By 1783, the Americans and British had a peace agreement. With the war over, some people expected George Washington to take over the United States. Some thought he might make himself a king. After all, he was the leader of the army. Who would stop him? But George Washington surprised them. He left his post, broke up the army, and returned to Mount Vernon.

Saying good-bye to his officers

◄ George Washington leaving the army

The First President

His much-loved Mount Vernon had suffered during the war. George spent four years repairing it. But soon, his country asked for his help again. The new country needed a new kind of government to survive.

To work out the details, leaders from each state went to Philadelphia for a meeting called the Constitutional Convention. The members

A view from the sky of Mount Vernon

asked George Washington to lead the meeting.

George Washington leading the Constitutional Convention

After the Constitution of the United States was signed, everyone wanted him to be president. On April 30, 1789, in New York City, George Washington became the first president of the United States.

Being sworn in as president

21

George Washington set an example for future presidents. He tried to stay out of arguments between groups of politicians. He believed that the United States should stay out of fights between other countries. He also helped plan the nation's new capital. It would be named Washington, in his honor.

The plan for the nation's capital city

◀ Pennsylvania Avenue in Washington, D.C.

He served two **terms** as president from 1789 to 1797. Then he decided not to run again.

Back at Mount Vernon

Once more, George Washington returned to Mount Vernon. He spent much of his time repairing the plantation. He also worked to build new barns and other buildings.

George designed these sixteen-sided barns at Mount Vernon.

◄ George Washington and his wife, Martha

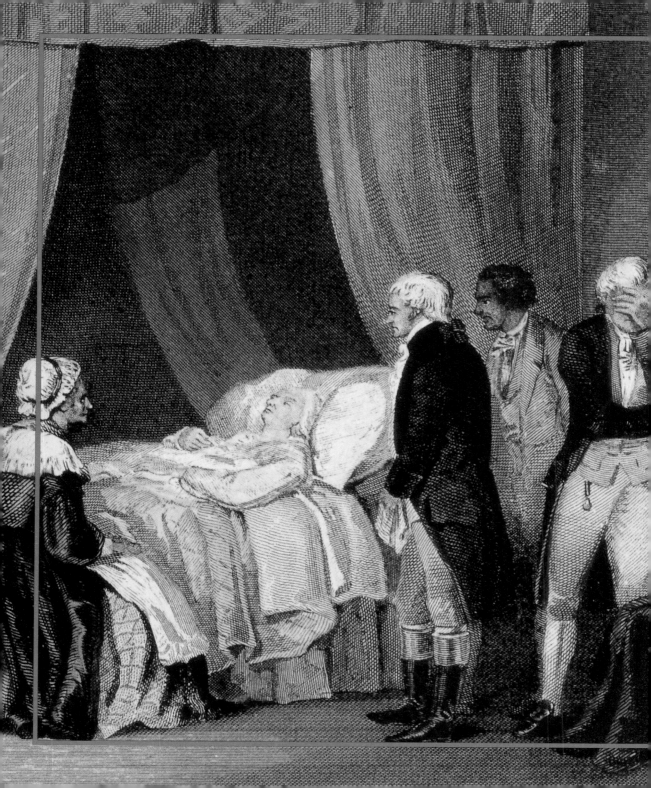

Two years later, in 1799, he caught a cold riding his horse in a rainstorm. His cold got worse, and he became very ill. On December 14, 1799, George Washington died.

He was buried at Mount Vernon. The entire nation was saddened by the loss of its first great leader. As Henry Lee said, George Washington was "first in war, first in peace and first in the hearts of his countrymen."

Important Dates in George Washington's Life

1732	Born on February 22 in Virginia
1743	George's father dies.
1749	Became a surveyor in Virginia
1754	Fights in the French and Indian War (1754–1763)
1759	Marries Martha Custis
1759	Is elected to the House of Burgesses in Virginia
1774	Serves in the First Continental Congress
1775	Serves in the Second Continental Congress
1775–1783	Serves as a general in the Revolutionary War
1789–1797	Serves as the first president of the United States
1799	Dies at Mount Vernon on December 14

Glossary

colony—an area that has been settled by people from another country and is controlled by that country

drilled—trained

mill—a building in which grain is ground into flour

settlers—people who live in a new place

surveyor—a person who measures the size and shape of a piece of land

terms—limited amounts of time

Did You Know?

- The popular story that young George Washington was so honest he admitted to his father that he had chopped a cherry tree is not true. George never cut down a cherry tree.

- George Washington's false teeth were made out of human and cow teeth and elephant ivory attached to a lead base.

- George Washington owned about 33,000 acres (13,365 hectares) in several states.

- George Washington is the only U.S. president to be elected by all the voters of the new country.

Want to Know More?

At the Library

Giblin, James, and Michael Dooling (illustrator). *George Washington: A Picture Book Biography.* New York: Scholastic, 1992.

Gross, Ruth Belov, and Emily Arnold McCully (illustrator). *If You Grew Up with George Washington.* New York: Scholastic, 1993.

On the Web

George Washington
http://www.history.org/people/washhdr.htm
For information about Washington's life

Mount Vernon Educational Resources
http://www.mountvernon.org/education/index.html
For information about George Washington and an online quiz

Through the Mail

The White House
1600 Pennsylvania Avenue, N.W.
Washington, DC 20500-0001
For information about the presidency

On the Road

George Washington's Mount Vernon Estate and Gardens
P.O. Box 110
Mount Vernon, VA 22121
703/780-2000
http://www.mountvernon.org/image/mtvernon.html
To visit George Washington's house and gardens

Index

About the Author
Andrew Santella is a writer in Chicago. He writes for a wide range of publications, including *Gentlemen's Quarterly*, the *New York Times Magazine*, and *Commonweal*. He is the author of several books for children on American history.